# Spotlight On
# Presentations

Jennifer Gipp

THOMSON
COURSE TECHNOLOGY

Australia • Canada • Mexico • Singapore • Spain • United Kingdom • United States

## Spotlight On Presentations
by Jennifer Gipp

**Executive Director, Learning Solutions:**
Nicole Jones Pinard

**Development Editors:**
David Rivera
Laurie Brown

**Senior Marketing Manager:**
Kim Ryttel

**Senior Acquisitions Editor:**
Jane Mazares

**School Market Specialist:**
Meagan Putney

**Product Managers:**
David Rivera
Sarah Santoro

**Editorial Assistant:**
Jeannine Lawless

**Director of Production:**
Patty Stephan

**Associate Production Manager:**
Aimee Poirier

**Senior Manufacturing Coordinator:**
Justin Palmeiro

**Manuscript Quality Assurance Lead:**
Burt LaFountain

**Interior Design:**
BIG BLUE DOT

**Cover Design:**
Laura Rickenbach

**Cover Image:**
Christopher Corr

**Copy Editor:**
Harry Johnson

**Proofreader:**
Christine Clark

**Indexer:**
Joan Green

**Compositor:**
GEX Publishing Services

# Table of Contents

# Preface

**Computer technology is on the move!** The advances can be seen and felt across society on a daily basis. As computer technology progresses, it is beginning to carve its path into the middle and elementary school levels. Though this is a scholastic discipline that is still very much in its infancy, it continues to advance and mold its importance in society.

Though many textbooks are dedicated to learners in high school or elementary school, it appears that our valued middle-school learners have been left out in the dark without a dedicated text. With this in mind, Thomson Course Technology is proud to present the *Spotlight On...* middle school product line.

With the commitment to our middle-school learners, we sought the authorship of an expert in grades 6–8. Jennifer Gipp is a computer technology middle-school teacher at D.C. Everest Middle School in Wisconsin. She has been teaching middle-school technology for the last three years and her proven lesson plans in the classroom are the foundation of this product line.

We at Thomson Course Technology recognize the importance of computer technology. In fact, we are dedicated to the progression and learning of computer technology as it makes its way to all levels of scholastic learning.

## OVERVIEW

The *Spotlight On...* product line introduces middle-school learners to basic technology concepts and skills through a computer application suite. With middle-school learners as the focal audience for this text, *Spotlight On...* has made efforts to keep the page count down, but not at the sacrifice of the essentials of computer concepts and tasks. Currently, the product line boasts an additional six titles:

> *Spotlight On Introduction to Computers*
> *Spotlight On Word Processing*
> *Spotlight On Spreadsheets*
> *Spotlight On Databases*
> *Spotlight On Multimedia*
> *Spotlight On the Internet*

The *Spotlight On...* product line is the perfect text for bridging elementary learning to the high school curriculum. This product line touts a series of features designed specifically for middle-school learners.

## CROSS-CURRICULAR ACTIVITIES

As time brings about change, so does technology. Currently, many states and districts have issued requirements for core disciplines to have a technological integration component. Knowing this, the *Spotlight On...* product line is committed to including substantial student projects that link technology to a core discipline. *Spotlight's* "Project Practice" touts at least four projects per chapter in the following subjects:

 Mathematics

 Science

 Language Arts

 Social Studies

 Music/Art

For *Spotlight On Presentations*, there are approximately 16 cross-curricular "Project Practices."

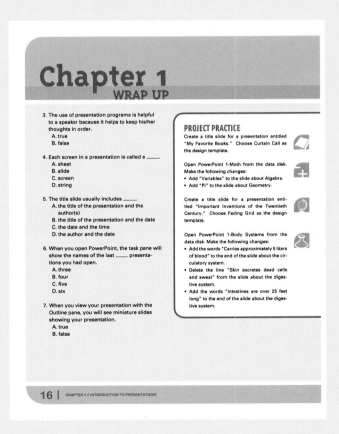

## STEP-BY-STEP INSTRUCTION

*Spotlight On...* strives to give students valuable computer concepts that are reinforced with step-by-step instruction. This product line is unique because of it balance between creating projects from scratch and making necessary edits and changes to data files and saving the files onto a computer or disk.

# Features

**In recent educational trends, parents have become more proactive in the involvement of their children's education.**

## PARENTAL INVOLVEMENT

In recent educational trends, parents have become more proactive in the involvement of their children's education. Though parents are the first and foremost educators of children, at times, publishers have moved away from parental involvement. The *Spotlight On...* series recognizes the importance of parental involvement and has dedicated one project per chapter within its texts to involve a parent or guardian's input. Though some households in the United States still do not have a computer, Jennifer Gipp customized these projects so that in most cases, a computer is not necessary for the parental projects. In many cases, the "Guided Practice" projects require the guidance and support of a parent or guardian.

## WORKING TOGETHER

The *Spotlight On...* product line encourages group projects within its text. Dubbed as the "Buddy Projects" within the end of chapter section, students are asked to work together in groups of two or three to accomplish fun tasks that are very much related to the everyday life of a middle-school learner. In each chapter, the *Spotlight On...* product line dedicates one project to the cooperation and accomplishments of group learning.

## MARGINAL FEATURES

Within each chapter, students can learn valuable information from *Spotlight's* marginal features. Being colorful and donning a picturesque icon, students will be drawn to the information within its boxes. *Spotlight's* marginal features include:

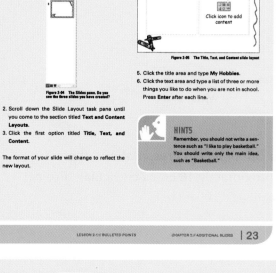

Tips and Tricks
- a means of showing students other ways to accomplish a task

Hint
- a reinforcement and reminder of valuable information learned in previous lessons.

Important Information
- information the student must know before tackling the task.

As part of our features, we also include a very special character. Because this text is a bridge between elementary and high-school learners, a support character has been added for those students that need just a little more guidance. P.D., an animated PDA (personal digital assistant), will help guide students as they explore the different computer application suites.

## KEY TERMS

The *Spotlight On...* product line knows the importance of good vocabulary building. Because of its importance, *Spotlight On...* includes dedicated sections for vocabulary terms on each page. Every lesson opens with a list of key terms. As the lesson continues, these key terms are defined in the Important Vocabulary Terms sections in the upper and lower margins of the book.

# ACKNOWLEDGEMENTS

In the creation of this book, the author would like to publicly thank the following individuals for their dedication to this new product line:

> My husband, Corey, and my children, Hunter and Olivia: thank you for your patience and understanding through the many late night of writing and editing.
> My 6th grade Computer Skills classes at D.C. Everest Middle School for helping me to understand what works and what doesn't for the middle-school learner.
> My high school business teacher, Marie C. Braatz: your dedication to students and enthusiasm for the business field are what inspired me to become a business teacher.
> Cheryl Costantini, VP of School Publishing and Marketing, and Jane Mazares, Sr. Acquisitions Editor: many thanks for bringing a dedicated text to the middle-school market and your confidence in me.
> Dave Rivera, Developmental Editor and Product Manager for the first four books: many thanks for being an integral part to publishing these books. Your insights will be greatly missed.
> Sarah Santoro, Product Manager, and Laurie Brown and Fran Marino, Developmental Editors for the final three books: thanks for stepping in to take care of the series after Dave's absence.
> Kim Ryttel, Sr. Marketing Manager, and Meagan Putney, School Market Specialist: thank you for your dedication to this product and spreading the word to our sales force. Your ingenuity for promoting these books is a valuable asset to us.
> Aimee Poirier, Associate Production Manager: thanks for keeping our books on schedule.
> Burt LaFountain, Manuscript QA Project Leader: I never knew so much work went into ensuring our product was at the highest quality. Thanks so much for the testing of materials.
> Laura Rickenbach, Graphic Designer: much gratitude to guiding the team through the different design ideas and your find for a cover illustrator.

# Dear Student,

Hello friend! Welcome to *Spotlight on Presentations*! In this book we will learn many things about presentation programs and how they have made our lives easier. We will learn how to create slides, insert clip art, motion clips, tables, and digital photos. We will add animation schemes and transitions to the slides to make them flow better. We will also add a variety of sounds to enhance the presentation.

I will be here throughout the textbook to help you learn about computers. I will show you examples of what your screen should look like, and I will also give you hints to help you remember some of the things we have done. I am a handheld computer, which is also called a personal digital assistant or PDA. You, my friend, can call me P.D.

Computers are used in nearly every part of our lives. I'm sure you cannot even imagine what life was like before computers. Try to imagine how much harder it would have been for some companies before the invention of computers and presentation software. You are very lucky to be learning this information now so you can use the knowledge today and in the future.

**YOUR FRIEND,**

**P.D.**

# Chapter 1

## INTRODUCTION TO PRESENTATIONS

**Have you ever given a presentation in front of your class and forgotten** what you were going to say? This problem could be eliminated with the use of an electronic presentation program such as PowerPoint. Students, teachers, sales executives, and business owners are just a few of the people that can benefit from the use of a PowerPoint presentation.

**IN THIS CHAPTER, WE WILL:**

> Learn about the uses of presentation software
> Look at the various parts of the presentation window
> Move around an existing presentation
> Open and edit an existing presentation
> Determine when to use Save and when to use Save As
> Print a handout
> Create a title slide
> Add a design template to our presentation

# Lesson 1-1 PRESENTATION BASICS

## IN THIS LESSON, WE WILL:
> Learn about the uses of presentation software
> Look at the various parts of the presentation window

## KEY TERMS
Formatting toolbar
menu bar
presentation program
slide
Standard toolbar
task pane
Title bar
title slide

Microsoft PowerPoint is an electronic **presentation program** that helps people present a speech using slides. The program benefits the speaker because it helps the presenter remember the presentation and keep thoughts or ideas in order. An electronic presentation program is also helpful to the audience. By both hearing and seeing the information, the audience can better retain important points in the presentation. The use of PowerPoint can also add pizzazz to the presentation through graphics such as clip art, photographs, and motion clips. Sounds can also be included to add emphasis to the presentation.

## PRESENTATION PROGRAM

Before electronic presentation programs like Microsoft PowerPoint, presenters had to print visual aids and copy them onto a clear sheet of plastic called transparency film. For the audience to view the visual aid, the sheet of transparency film needed to be placed on top of an overhead projector.

Figure 1-01    A speaker using transparency film and an overhead projector to give a presentation

1. Log in to your computer if you haven't already.
2. Find the Microsoft PowerPoint icon on your desktop.
3. Double-click the icon to open the program.

### IMPORTANT INFORMATION
If you do not see a shortcut on your desktop to open Microsoft PowerPoint, you can click **Start** at the bottom-left of your screen, go to **All Programs**, find **Microsoft Office**, and then click **Microsoft Office PowerPoint 2003**.

## IMPORTANT VOCABULARY TERMS

**presentation program:** software that acts like an electronic outline used to present information.

You will see a screen displaying an entire sheet of paper. This sheet of paper is called a **slide**, and it is used to display information. The first slide you will see is called a title slide and has two text boxes on it: one that says "Click to add title" and one that says "Click to add subtitle." This is a great way to remember to always add a title slide to your presentation. The **title slide** is generally the first slide of your presentation, and it is used to tell the title of the presentation and the author(s). The title slide of a presentation is very similar to the cover of a book.

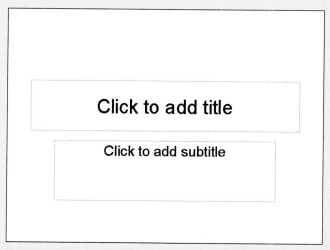

**Figure 1-02   A blank title slide**

# PARTS OF THE WINDOW

When you open PowerPoint, your computer will begin preparing a blank presentation, starting with the title slide. Before we start entering any information, let's take a look at the other parts of the window.

## IMPORTANT INFORMATION

All screen shots are from Microsoft PowerPoint 2003. Your screen might look a little different if you are using a different version of this program.

When you open Microsoft PowerPoint, you will also see a **task pane** called "Getting Started" along the right side of the screen. In this task pane, you can connect to Microsoft Office Online, get help, open an existing presentation, or create a new presentation. You will also see a list of the last four documents that you had open. The task pane area will also be used for many other tasks such as adding clip art or changing the slide layout or slide design.

**slide:** a screen in an electronic presentation program used to display information.

**title slide:** generally the first slide of a presentation used to tell the title of the presentation and the author(s).

**task pane:** part of the window that is used to open an existing presentation, to create a new presentation, and for searching.

# Lesson 1-1 PRESENTATION BASICS

If the task pane does not appear, you can click View on the menu located at the top of your screen and select Task Pane to open it.

## POWERPOINT TOOLBARS

The blue bar that runs across the top of the screen that tells the name of the document as well as the name of the program is called the **Title bar**. The Title bar also contains the Minimize, Maximize/ Restore Down, and Close buttons.

Figure 1-03    The task pane

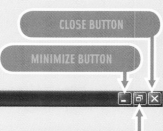

Figure 1-04    The Title bar

Below the Title bar is a row of words. These words make up the **menu bar**. When you click each word, a list of other commands will appear. All formatting can be done through the Menu bar.

Figure 1-05    The menu bar

You also have two toolbars across the top of your screen. The first toolbar is called the **Standard toolbar**, and it contains shortcuts for many common tools such as Open, Save, Print, and View. The first button on this toolbar is the "New" button; it looks like a little piece of paper.

Figure 1-06    The Standard toolbar

The next toolbar is called the **Formatting toolbar**. It contains many shortcuts for changing the appearance of your text such as the font, size, and color. The first button on the Formatting toolbar is the "font" drop-down button.

**Figure 1-07   The Formatting toolbar**

When you place your pointer over the buttons on any of the toolbars, you will get a small pop-up label indicating what that button does. We will use many of the tools on the Standard and Formatting toolbars throughout this book. If you do not see either of these toolbars, you can click View and then click Toolbars on the Menu bar. You will see a list of all available toolbars. Click the one(s) that you need to display them.

*To find out what each button on the toolbar does, place your mouse pointer over the button. You will see a little box appear telling you what that button is used for.*

## TIPS & TRICKS
Another way to display any missing toolbars is to right-click in the light-blue area at the top of the screen. You will see a list of all available toolbars. Click the one(s) that you need.

## NOW YOU TRY IT!
Take some time to explore the Standard and Formatting toolbars found across the top of your screen. Place your pointer over each button and find out what each button does.

# Lesson 1-2 MOVING AROUND

While we would like to get started working with our presentation, we should ensure that we're sitting at our computer correctly. Here are some important points you need to remember while you are keying:

- Sit up straight.
- Keep your feet on the floor.
- Keep your fingers on home row.
- Keep your elbows resting comfortably at your sides.
- Keep your wrists straight and your palms off the keyboard or the table.
- Keep your eyes on your copy (not on your fingers).
- Keep your keyboard at the edge of the table or desk.

*Home row is the middle row of letters on your keyboard. Your index fingers should be resting on the F and the J keys. When you type, your fingers should reach to the other letters and then come back to home row.*

## MOVING AROUND

1. Open **Microsoft PowerPoint** if it is not already open.

Next, you need to open a file from the data disk. When you open PowerPoint, the task pane will show the last four presentations that have been opened on your computer. If you see the name of the file you are looking for, you could just click the file's name. However, because this is probably the first time you have used PowerPoint, you will need to click the More... option at the bottom of the task pane that has a folder icon next to it.

2. On the task pane, click **More...** to open an existing presentation.

**Figure 1-08    The More... option on the task pane**

## TIPS & TRICKS

If you cannot see the task pane, you can also choose **File** and **New** to open the New Presentation task pane.

The Open dialog box appears. Your teacher will tell you where you can access the data files.

3. Open the file **PowerPoint 1-Extracurricular Activities** from the data disk.

When you open the file, you will see the title page of the presentation.

Before you continue, save the file with a different name.

4. Click the word **File** on the menu bar to show its drop-down menu.

Because you have opened a file from the data disk, you want to save it with a different name. The original file will stay intact.

5. Click **Save As**.

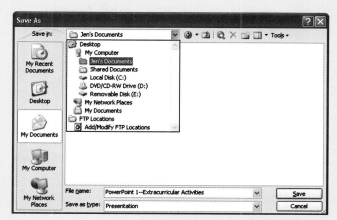

Figure 1-09    The Save As dialog box

The only time you need to use the Save As option is when you want to change the name or location of a document and you still want to keep the original document intact. If you have already saved a document and you click Save, the file will be saved with the same name and location as you previously chose. You will not see a window asking for a filename or saving location. Don't worry, it still saves.

At the top of the window, you will see a drop-down arrow next to the words Save In.

6. Click the drop-down arrow and click your folder on the network. Your teacher will tell you to what drive you should be saving.

# Lesson 1-2 MOVING AROUND

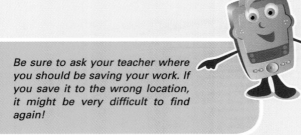

*Be sure to ask your teacher where you should be saving your work. If you save it to the wrong location, it might be very difficult to find again!*

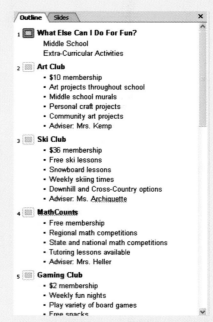

**Figure 1-10   The Outline pane**

7. In the File name text box, type **PowerPoint 1.2-Edits**.
8. Click the **Save** button.

## EDITING THE PRESENTATION

Along the left side of the screen, we have two options to view our presentation: Outline view and Slides view.

These two views can be selected by clicking the tab at the top of the pane. The **Outline tab** will show the presentation as a traditional outline, with bulleted points. This is very similar to an outline that you would create on paper when planning your presentation. If you click anywhere in the outline, you will see the larger image of that slide on your screen.

The other option to view the presentation is through the **Slides tab**. The Slides pane option will show small pictures of each slide as it will appear. If you click any of the small slide pictures, the larger image of the slide will appear on the screen. These two options are very helpful when editing your presentation, because they provide an easy way to move around and see the final layout.

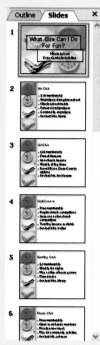

Figure 1-11 The Slides tab

**IMPORTANT INFORMATION**

You can select a single word by double-clicking it with your mouse.

You can select an entire line by triple-clicking it with your mouse.

4. Type **$1** in its place.
5. Click slide number **5** to select it.

**TIPS & TRICKS**

You can also press the Page Up and Page Down buttons located on the right side of your keyboard to move around a presentation.

Before we can show this presentation, we need to make some changes.

1. Click the **Slides** tab to view the entire presentation as mini slides, if it is not already that way.
2. Click slide number **8** once to view it. You might need to use the scroll bars to get to the slide. The Fitness Club information should appear.

The Fitness Club has decided to charge a $1 annual membership fee.

3. Select the word **"Free"** in the first row.

The Gaming Club has decided to increase its annual membership fee.

6. Select the word **"2"** in the first row.
7. Type **3** in its place.
8. View slide number **9** using either your Page Up and Page Down buttons or by clicking the mini slide number 9 at the left side of the screen.

The adviser has changed for the Homework Club.

9. Select **Mrs. Oboikovitz**.
10. Type **Mr. Rivera** in its place.
11. View slide number **4** using either your Page Up and Page Down buttons or by clicking the mini slide number 4 at the left side of the screen.

The adviser has changed for the Math Club.

12. Select **Mrs. Heller**.
13. Type **Miss Yang** in its place.
14. Click the **Save** button on the Standard toolbar (the button looks like a little disk) to save your work.

## TIPS & TRICKS

You can also save your work by clicking **File** and **Save** or by holding down the **Ctrl** key and pressing the letter **S**.

## ADDING INFORMATION TO THE SLIDES

Some clubs have decided to add a little more information to their slides for the assembly.

1. View slide number **2** using either your Page Up and Page Down buttons or by clicking the mini slide number 2 at the left side of the screen.

The Art Club adviser wants to add a little more information about community projects.

2. Click at the end of the **fourth** line.
3. Press **Enter** to create a blank line with a bullet.

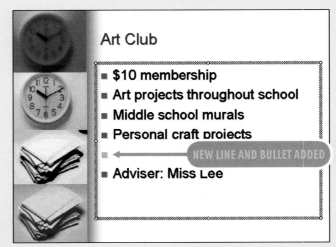

Figure 1-12   Screen snapshot

4. Type **Community art projects**.
5. View slide number **5** using either your Page Up and Page Down buttons or by clicking the mini slide number 5 at the left side of the screen.

The Gaming Club has decided to add monthly tournaments.

6. Click at the end of the **third** line.
7. Press **Enter** to create a blank line with a bullet.

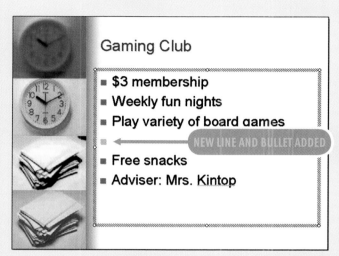

Gaming Club

- $3 membership
- Weekly fun nights
- Play variety of board games
- [NEW LINE AND BULLET ADDED]
- Free snacks
- Adviser: Mrs. Kintop

**Figure 1-13    Screen snapshot**

8. Type **Monthly tournaments**.
9. Save your work again.

# PRINTING

Because this presentation will be shared at a middle school kick-off assembly, it would be nice to have handouts on which students can take notes.

1. Click **File** on the menu bar and then click **Print**.
2. Click the drop-down arrow next to **Print what:** and then click **Handouts**.
3. Click the drop-down arrow next to **Slides per page** and then click **3**.

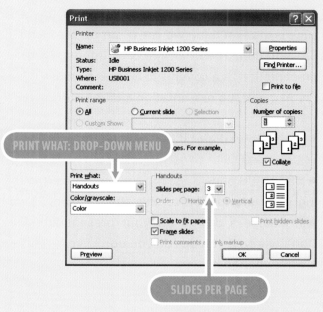

**Figure 1-14    The Print dialog box**

4. Click the **OK** button.

## NOW YOU TRY IT!

Open the file PowerPoint 1-FBLA from the data disk. Make the following changes:

- On slide 3, remove the last line that says "Leadership conferences" because it is repeated.
- Add the line "Holiday gift donations" at the bottom of the fourth slide.
- Add the words "Impromptu and rehearsed" before "speaking" in the first line on the second slide.

Save the file as **Now You Try It-Lesson 1.2**.

# Lesson 1-3 CREATING A SLIDE

## IN THIS LESSON, WE WILL:
> Create a title slide
> Add a design template to our presentation

## KEY TERMS
design template

As we learned in the previous lessons, the title slide is the first thing we see when we start a blank presentation. The title slide is as important to our presentation as a cover is to a book, because it tells the name of the presentation and the author(s).

1. Open **PowerPoint** if it is not already open.

A blank title page appears. You could start entering your information on this sheet; however, you will choose a design for your presentation first. Don't worry, if you decide you don't like it, you can always change it later.

2. On the task pane, click **Create a new presentation**.

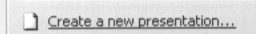

**Figure 1-15** The Create a new presentation option on the task pane

**Figure 1-16** The New Presentation task pane

## NEW PRESENTATION

In the New Presentation task pane, you have the choice to create a new blank presentation, a presentation from the design template, a presentation from the AutoContent wizard, a presentation from an existing presentation, or a new photo album.

If you were to choose the blank presentation, you really wouldn't need to use the New Presentation task pane because PowerPoint automatically starts a blank presentation when the program is opened.

## TIPS & TRICKS

If you cannot see the task pane, you can also click **File** on the menu bar and then click **New** to open the New Presentation task pane.

**design template:** preset background design with coordinating text.

A presentation started from the **design template** gives you many options for the design of your presentation. Approximately 25 design backgrounds are already loaded with your program to give you a variety of designs for your presentation. When you choose a design template, there is a background design with coordinating text already formatted for you. For this lesson, we will choose the design template option, but first let's find out when we would want to use the other options available on this task pane.

When you would like some help determining the design and style of your presentation, you use the AutoContent wizard. This option takes you through a series of questions to help customize your presentation for your given audience. This wizard also provides ideas and an organization for your presentation. The wizard gives suggestions for presentations from selling a product or service and recommending a strategy to a presentation for a company meeting. When using the AutoContent wizard, you also are given suggestions as to what types of information you should include in your presentation.

Another option on the New Presentation task pane is to open an existing presentation. You use this option when you want to access a presentation you have already created. This is helpful when you want to make some changes to a presentation or add some additional slides, but still keep the original presentation intact.

The final option is to create a new photo album. You can use Microsoft PowerPoint to easily create a presentation as a photo album if you simply want to add a large group of your favorite pictures to a presentation without the hassle of customizing each picture. PowerPoint allows you to add multiple pictures from your hard disk, scanner, digital camera, or Web camera to your photo album.

## THE TITLE SLIDE

1. Click **From design template** on the New Presentation task pane.
2. This presentation will be about you, so scroll down until you find the design template titled **Crayons**. Click the template once to select it for our presentation.

# Lesson 1-3 CREATING A SLIDE

The title slide will have changed to reflect the new design. The font has also changed.

**Figure 1-17    The title slide formatted with the Crayons design template**

*The great thing about choosing a design template is that you have a design combination that is easy to read. You do not need to change the color or the font.*

3. Click where it says "Click to add title" and type **All About Me**.
4. Click where it says "Click to add subtitle" and type **By:** and your name.

Great job! We are off to a good start on our presentation. We are going to finish the presentation in the next chapter. Let's save our work first.

5. Click **File** on the menu bar and then click **Save**. Make sure you are saving to your folder on the server.
6. Save the file as **PowerPoint 1.3-About Me**.

## NOW YOU TRY IT!
Create a title slide for a presentation titled Information about Pennsylvania (substitute the name of your state for "Pennsylvania"). Choose Slit as the design template. Save the file as **Now You Try It-Lesson 1.3**.

# Chapter 1
## WRAP UP

> Presentation programs act like an electronic outline used to present information.
> Graphics such as clip art, photographs, and motion clips can be added to a presentation to aid in comprehension and add interest.
> Sounds can also be added to a presentation to add emphasis.
> Presentation programs help the speaker by keeping his or her thoughts in order and helping him or her remember the presentation.
> Presentation programs help the audience members remember the information presented because they not only hear it, but they also see it. It is also usually much more interesting to listen to a presentation when there are visual aids.
> Each screen in an electronic presentation is called a slide.
> The Page Up and Page Down buttons move you from slide to slide within a presentation.
> PowerPoint has the capability to print handouts for audience members to follow along easily with the presentation.
> A design template can be added to a presentation to add a colorful background with coordinating text.

## WHAT DO YOU KNOW?

1. A presentation program is computer software that can be used to type and edit reports, letters, and tables.
   - A. true
   - B. false

2. _____ can be added to a presentation to add interest and aid in comprehension.
   - A. Clip art
   - B. Photographs
   - C. Motion clips
   - D. all of the above

# Chapter 1
## WRAP UP

3. The use of presentation programs is helpful to a speaker because it helps to keep his or her thoughts in order.
   A. true
   B. false

4. Each screen in a presentation is called a _____.
   A. sheet
   B. slide
   C. screen
   D. string

5. The title slide usually includes _____.
   A. the title of the presentation and the author(s)
   B. the title of the presentation and the date
   C. the date and the time
   D. the author and the date

6. When you open PowerPoint, the task pane will show the names of the last _____ presentations you had open.
   A. three
   B. four
   C. five
   D. six

7. When you view your presentation with the Outline tab, you will see miniature slides showing your presentation.
   A. true
   B. false

## PROJECT PRACTICE

Create a title slide for a presentation titled "My Favorite Books." Choose Curtain Call as the design template.

Open PowerPoint 1-Math from the data disk. Make the following changes:
- Add a bullet and the word "Variables" to the slide about algebra.
- Add a bullet and the word "Pi" to the slide about geometry.

Create a title slide for a presentation titled "Important Inventions of the Twentieth Century." Choose Fading Grid as the design template.

Open PowerPoint 1-Body Systems from the data disk. Make the following changes:
- Add a bullet and the words "Carries approximately 5 liters of blood" to the end of the slide about the circulatory system.
- Delete the bullet and the line "Skin excretes dead cells and sweat" from the slide about the digestive system.
- Add a bullet and the words "Intestines are over 25 feet long" to the end of the slide about the digestive system.

8. What is one way to create a new presentation?
   A. Click "Create a new presentation" on the task pane.
   B. Click "Open a new file" on the task pane.
   C. Click "Make a new document" on the task pane.
   D. Click "Design a new slide" on the task pane.

9. If you want to add a decorative background with coordinating text to your presentation, you should choose _____ from the New Presentation task pane.
   A. Blank Presentation
   B. From Design Template
   C. From AutoContent Wizard
   D. From Existing Presentation

10. The _____ wizard gives you suggested layouts and information for your presentation.
    A. AutoFormat
    B. AutoCorrect
    C. AutoContent
    D. AutoFill

11. You can create a photo album in Microsoft PowerPoint.
    A. true
    B. false

## BUDDY PROJECT

Work with a partner or group of three to create a title slide for a decade of your choice. Choose a design template and add a creative title.

## GUIDED PRACTICE

Talk with your parent or guardian about possible career choices for you when you get older. Create a title slide using the name of your chosen career. Choose a design template that you like.

12. If you would like some help determining the design and style of your presentation, you should choose _____ from the New Presentation task pane.
    A. Open Existing Presentation
    B. Photo Album
    C. From AutoContent Wizard
    D. From Design Template

13. If you want to view your slide show as miniature slides along the left side of the screen, you should choose the _____ tab.
    A. Miniature
    B. Screen
    C. Outline
    D. Slide

14. PowerPoint automatically starts a blank presentation when the program is opened.
    A. true
    B. false

15. If you cannot see the New Presentation task pane, you can click _____ to open it.
    A. File and then click New
    B. Edit and then click New
    C. View and then click New
    D. Insert and then click New

# Chapter 2
## ADDITIONAL SLIDES

**Have you ever been to a museum? Many times, you can attend a** presentation at a museum about a historical period, a famous artist, or even the life of a dinosaur. These presentations may contain visual aids such as charts and tables to help better describe the subject.

**IN THIS CHAPTER, WE WILL:**
> Learn the 7x7 rule
> Create slides using bullets
> Add clip art to a slide
> Make an organization chart on a slide
> Insert a table onto a slide
> Insert a media clip onto a slide
> Add a digital photo to a slide

# Lesson 2-1 BULLETED POINTS

## IN THIS LESSON, WE WILL:
> Learn the 7x7 rule
> Create slides using bullets
> Add clip art to a slide

## KEY TERMS
7x7 rule
bullets
clip art

When you are making a list, you probably make a little dash, dot, or little pictures before the word or words you are writing on the list. These dots, dashes, or little pictures are called **bullets** and they should be consistent within the list. Bullets are lined up vertically at the left.

As we learned in the last chapter, a PowerPoint presentation is very similar to an outline indicating the major points of our presentation. You should not type paragraphs or even sentences in PowerPoint. The rule to remember when preparing a PowerPoint presentation is that you should never have more than seven words next to a bullet. Also, you should have seven or fewer bulleted items on a single slide. This is called the **7x7 rule**. If you find that you are going to exceed this number, just break the information into two or more slides.

1. Open Microsoft PowerPoint.
2. Open the file **PowerPoint 1.3-About Me** that you created in the last chapter.

3. To change the name of the file, while still keeping the original file intact, click the **Save As** option under **File** on the menu bar.
4. Save the file as **PowerPoint 2.1-About Me**.

You should see the title slide that we created in the last chapter. We will add all of our slides to this presentation.

## TITLE AND TEXT LAYOUT

The first slide we will create will have a title and text formatted as a bulleted list. This layout is called "Title and Text" and is the default setting when you create a new slide.

1. Click **Insert** on the menu bar and then click **New Slide**.

You should now see a new slide on your screen automatically formatted with the title and text layout.

## IMPORTANT VOCABULARY TERMS

**bullets:** small dots, dashes, or other pictures used when creating lists. They should be consistent within the list.

**7x7 rule:** no more than seven bullets on a slide and no more than seven words within each bulleted point.

Figure 2-01    A new slide formatted as Title and Text

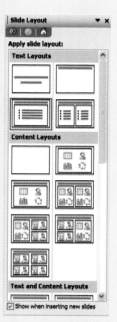

Figure 2-02    The Slide Layout task pane

Because this is the layout we want to use, we don't need to do anything else. However, if we did want to change the layout, we could use the Slide Layout task pane at the right side of your screen.

2. Click your slide where it says "Click to add title."
3. Type **Biography**.
4. Click your slide where it says "Click to add text."
5. On the first line, type your birthday.
6. Press **Enter**.

You will notice that another bullet has been created for you to continue your list.

7. On the second line, type the name of the city and state where you were born.
8. Press **Enter** to go to the third line.
9. Type the name of the elementary school you attended.

# Lesson 2-1 BULLETED POINTS

## HINTS

If you attended more than one elementary school, please list each one on a separate line, starting with the last elementary school you attended.

*If you have attended more than four elementary schools, that's okay. Just list the four most recent elementary schools you attended so we can still follow the 7x7 rule.*

10. Press **Enter** to go to the next line.
11. Type the name of the school you currently attend.

That's it! We have completed our first slide.

12. Save your work.

## TITLE, TEXT, AND CLIP ART

We want to create another new slide. This time we will use our toolbar.

1. Click the **New Slide** button on the Formatting toolbar.

NEW SLIDE BUTTON

**Figure 2-03 The New Slide button on the Formatting toolbar**

A new Title and Text slide appears on your screen. If you look at the pane along the left side of your screen, you will see that you now have three slides.

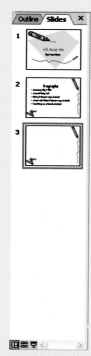

Figure 2-04    The Slides pane. Do you
see the three slides you have created?

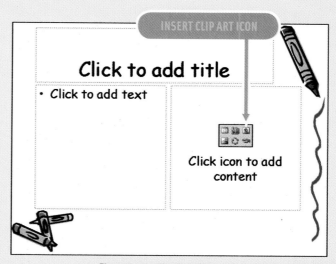

Figure 2-05    The Title, Text, and Content slide layout

4. Click the title area and type **My Hobbies**.

5. Click the text area and type a list of three or more things you like to do when you are not in school. Press **Enter** after each line.

2. Scroll down the Slide Layout task pane until you come to the section titled **Text and Content Layouts**.

3. Click the first option titled **Title, Text, and Content**.

The format of your slide will change to reflect the new layout.

## HINTS

Remember, you should not write a sentence such as "I like to play basketball." You should write only the main idea, such as "Basketball."

# Lesson 2-1 BULLETED POINTS

**clip art:** drawing of
an object used to add
emphasis to text.

In the content area of the slide, you could insert several items, such as: a table, chart, clip art, picture, diagram or organization chart, or media clip.

Now, we will insert a piece of clip art. **Clip art** is a drawing of an object used to add emphasis to text in a document or presentation.

6. Click the **Insert Clip Art** icon on the slide.

7. Scroll through the items displayed in the Select Picture dialog box to find a piece of clip art that will relate to your list of hobbies.

8. Click the picture. Click the **OK** button to insert the picture.

9. Save your work again and close PowerPoint.

Figure 2-06   The Select Picture dialog box

## NOW YOU TRY IT!

Open the Now You Try It exercise from Lesson 1.3 in Chapter 1. You will add a slide about the history of your state. Using your social studies book, the Internet, or the library, research your state's statehood. Format your slide with Title and Text. Type Statehood as the title. List the year, the founders, and the state's first city on your slide. Save your work as **Now You Try It-Lesson 2.1**.

# Lesson 2-2 TABLES AND CHARTS

## IN THIS LESSON, WE WILL:
> **Make an organization chart on a slide**
> **Insert a table on a slide**

## KEY TERMS
**cell**
**organization chart**
**table**

Sometimes, we want to display information on a slide in a format that is different from a bulleted list. We could choose to compare items in a table or show the relationship of items in an organization chart.

## ORGANIZATION CHART

In this lesson, we will use the organization chart to show the members of our family. An **organization chart** is used to show the hierarchical relationship of items.

1. Open Microsoft PowerPoint.
2. Use the task pane to open **PowerPoint 2.1-About Me**.
3. If you do not see the task pane, click **View** on the menu bar and then click **Task Pane**.

Because PowerPoint 2.1-About Me was probably one of the last four presentations you opened, you should see it at the bottom of the Getting Started task pane. You can just click the name of the file, and it will open.

## TIPS & TRICKS
You could also open the file by clicking **File** and then clicking **Open** or by clicking the **Open** button on the Standard toolbar. Another way to open the file is by holding down the **Ctrl** key and pressing the letter **O**.

4. Save the file as **PowerPoint 2.2-About Me**.
5. Insert a new slide using one of the ways we learned in the last lesson.

Oops! Because we were currently viewing the first slide, the newly inserted slide appeared as the second slide. We can verify this by viewing the Slides tab along the left side of the screen. Don't worry, we will move that slide right now to where it belongs.

## IMPORTANT VOCABULARY TERMS

**organization chart:** diagram used to show the hierarchical relationship of items.

# Lesson 2-2 TABLES AND CHARTS

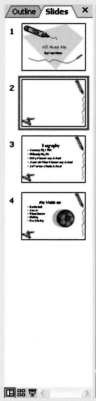

Figure 2-07    The Slides tab

Figure 2-08    The Insert Diagram or Organization Chart icon

The Diagram Gallery dialog box opens, giving you a choice of six different diagrams: organization chart, cycle, radial, pyramid, Venn, and target diagrams.

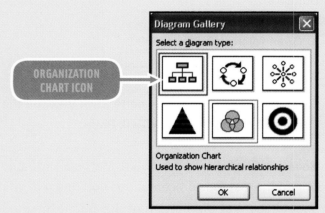

Figure 2-09    The Diagram Gallery dialog box

6. Click and hold the second slide. Drag it to the bottom of the list and let go. It should now appear as slide number four.
7. On the Slide Layout task pane, scroll down to the **Content Layouts** section. Click the **Title and Content** option.
8. Click in the title area and type **My Family**.
9. In the content area, click the **Insert Diagram or Organization Chart** icon.

10. Click the **Organization Chart** option and then click the **OK** button.

An organization chart is created on the slide with one major text box and three subordinate text boxes. We will add or delete the subordinate text boxes a little later.

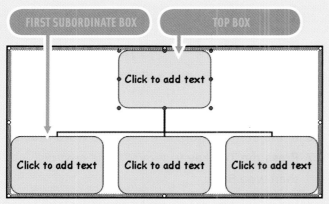

**Figure 2-10  The Organization chart**

11. Click the top box and then type the name(s) of your parent(s) or guardian(s).
12. Click the first subordinate box and then type the name of your oldest sibling. If you are the oldest, type your name here.
13. Click the next subordinate box and then type the name of your next-oldest sibling.
14. Continue to type the name of your next sibling.
15. If you need to add another subordinate text box for another sibling, click the down arrow next to the **Insert Shape** button on the Organization Chart toolbar.

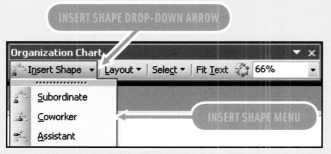

**Figure 2-11  The Insert Shape button and drop-down menu on the Organization Chart toolbar**

**table:** diagram with columns and rows used to list and compare items.

**cell:** each individual box of a table.

16. Click **Co-Worker.**
17. Continue to add text boxes until you have enough to list all of your siblings.
18. If you need to delete some of the subordinate text boxes, you can right-click the text box and then click **delete** from the drop-down menu.

If you have a lot of siblings, you may want to experiment with the layout. Click the Layout button on the Organization Chart toolbar to see the available options.

*We all know that families come in all shapes and sizes. Don't worry if your diagram does not look like your neighbor's.*

19. Save your work.

# TABLE

We are going to continue working with the presentation we just created to add one more slide. This time we will use a table to list several items. **Tables** are diagrams with columns and rows used to list and compare items. Each individual box of a table is called a **cell**.

# Lesson 2-2 TABLES AND CHARTS

1. Insert a new slide using one of the ways you learned earlier.

2. From the Slide Layout task pane, click the **Title and Content** layout under the Content Layouts subheading.
3. Click the title area and type **My Favorites**.
4. In the content area, click the **Insert Table** icon.

INSERT TABLE ICON

**Figure 2-12    The Insert Table icon on the slide**

The Insert Table dialog box appears, asking how many columns and rows you would like in your table.

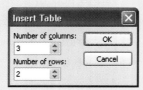

**Figure 2-13    The Insert Table dialog box**

5. Type **3** for the Number of columns and **2** for the Number of rows and then click the **OK** button.

A table appears on your slide with three columns and two rows.

6. In the first cell (top, left), type the word **Movie**.
7. Press the **Tab** key to move to the next cell and then type **Book**.
8. Press the **Tab** key to move to the next cell and then type **Food**.
9. Press the **Tab** key again to move to the first cell of the second row.
10. Type the name of your favorite movie.
11. Press the **Tab** key to move to the next cell and type the name of your favorite book.
12. Press the **Tab** key to move to the last cell and type your favorite food.
13. Save your work and close PowerPoint.

## NOW YOU TRY IT!
Open the file about your state you began working on in the Now You Try It exercise of the last lesson. Insert a new slide containing a table with four columns and two rows. Title the slide State Symbols. In the top row, type Animal, Flower, Rock, Bird. Use the reference books in the library to find out your state's animal, flower, rock, and bird. Fill in the cells with the information. Save the file as **Now You Try It-Lesson 2.2**.

# Lesson 2-3 PHOTOS AND MEDIA CLIPS

IN THIS LESSON, WE WILL:
> Insert a media clip onto a slide
> Add a digital photo to a slide

KEY TERMS
media clip

In this lesson, we want to add a few more visual pieces to our presentation by inserting a personal photo and a media clip. In PowerPoint, a **media clip** can be an actual clip of a movie, but it can also be animated clip art.

1. Open Microsoft PowerPoint if it is not already open.
2. Use the task pane to open **PowerPoint 2.2-About Me**.
3. If you do not see the task pane, click **View** on the menu bar and then click **Task Pane**.

## MEDIA CLIP

Because PowerPoint 2.2-About Me was probably one of the last four presentations you opened, you should see it at the bottom of the task pane. You can just click the name of the file, and it will open.

1. Save the file as **PowerPoint 2.3-About Me**.
2. Press the **Page Down** button until slide number 5, which shows the table of favorites, is selected.

3. Insert a new slide using one of the ways you learned in the last lesson.

The slide will contain a media clip of animated clip art.

4. Change the slide layout to **Title, Text, and Content** from the Slide Layout task pane.
5. Click the title area and then type **Future Career Plans**.
6. Click the **Insert Media Clip** icon on the slide.

INSERT MEDIA CLIP ICON

**Figure 2-14   The Insert Media Clip icon**

The Media Clip dialog box opens.

IMPORTANT VOCABULARY TERMS

**media clip:** animated clip art or actual clip from a movie.

LESSON 2-3:// PHOTOS AND MEDIA CLIPS          CHAPTER 2:// ADDITIONAL SLIDES    | 29

# Lesson 2-3 PHOTOS AND MEDIA CLIPS

**Figure 2-15 The Media Clip dialog box**

7. This slide is about your future career. Click the search box, type a word that relates to your future career plan, and then click the **Go** button.

8. Click a media clip that relates to the career plan and click the **OK** button to insert it.

9. Click the text area. At the first bulleted point, type your career choice.

10. Press **Enter** to start a new bulleted point.

11. Type two or three more items about the career, pressing **Enter** after each one.

12. Save your work.

## DIGITAL PHOTO

We want to add a personal photo to our final slide. If you have a digital camera, you can use that to take a photograph of yourself. Because digital cameras are all so different, you will need to find out how to load the photos from your camera to your computer.

*Ask your teacher how to load your digital photos to your computer if you don't know how.*

## ! IMPORTANT INFORMATION
Your media clip will not play until you view your slide show.

1. Make sure slide number 6 is selected.
2. Insert a new slide using one of the ways you learned in Lesson 2-1.

The slide will contain a photo and a title.

3. Change the slide layout to **Title and Content**.
4. Click the title area and type **Thanks for Watching!**
5. Click the **Insert Picture** icon on the slide.

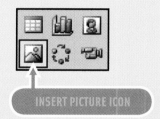

Figure 2-16    The Insert Picture icon

The Insert Picture dialog box opens.

Clicking the Insert Picture icon allows you to insert any photo, clip art, or graphic that you have saved to your computer besides those that are loaded into your clip organizer.

6. Click the down arrow next to the Look In box. Click the folder where your photo is saved.
7. Click the photo and then click the **Insert** button.
8. Save your work again.

## NOW YOU TRY IT!

Create an informational slide with a motion clip formatted with the Title, Text, and Content layout. Include information regarding Red Ribbon Week that could be used at a school assembly. Save your file as **Now You Try It-Lesson 2.3**.

# Chapter 2
## WRAP UP

> Main ideas can be shown on a slide in a bulleted list.
> Bullets are small dots or other pictures used when creating lists.
> Bullets should be consistent within the list, and should be left aligned.
> PowerPoint presentations should not contain paragraphs or long sentences.
> The 7x7 rule states that there should not be more than seven bullets on a slide and no more than seven words within each bulleted point.
> The default PowerPoint slide layout is Title and Text.
> Slides can contain objects such as: a table, chart, clip art, picture, diagram or organization chart, or media clip.

## WHAT DO YOU KNOW?

1. Bullets should be lined up at the right side of the slide.
    A. true
    B. false

2. Bullets should be consistent within a list.
    A. true
    B. false

3. The 7x7 rule states that _____ .
    A. you should always have seven bulleted points on each slide with seven words within each bullet
    B. you should have fewer than seven bulleted points on each slide with exactly seven words within each bullet
    C. you should have no more than seven bulleted points on each slide with no more than seven words in each bullet
    D. none of the above

4. The default slide layout is the _____ layout.
   A. Title and Text
   B. Title, Text, and Content
   C. Content Only
   D. Text Only

5. The shortcut to insert a new slide is _____.
   A. Shift + M
   B. Ctrl + M
   C. Alt + M
   D. Ctrl + N

6. A(n) _____ is used to show the hierarchical relationship of items.
   A. Venn diagram
   B. target diagram
   C. pyramid diagram
   D. organization chart

7. A(n) _____ has columns and rows and is used to list and compare items.
   A. cycle diagram
   B. organization chart
   C. table
   D. radial diagram

8. A media clip can be an actual clip of a movie or a(n) _____.
   A. piece of still clip art
   B. animated piece of clip art
   C. digital photo
   D. sound clip

## CROSS-CURRICULAR PROJECT

Open the file you created in the last chapter titled "My Favorite Books." Add three slides using Title, Text, and Content. For each slide, write the title of a book as the title. For the text, write the name of the main character(s), the location, and a little about the plot. Add relevant clip art for each slide.

Create a slide with a table with four columns and three rows. List the main concepts you are learning in your math class in the top row. In the two rows beneath each concept, type a formula that you have used in this concept.

Open the file you created in the last chapter titled "Important Inventions of the Twentieth Century." Add four slides using Title, Text, and Content. For each slide, write the invention as the title. For the text, write the name of the inventor(s), the year, and how the invention affects society today. Add relevant clip art for each slide.

Create a slide using an organization chart. Use this chart to help explain a process you are currently learning about in science, such as how weather patterns and rain occur, or how and why a reptile sheds its skin.

9. Press the _____ key to move forward one slide at a time.
   - A. Page Down
   - B. Page Up
   - C. Backspace
   - D. Tab

10. Media clips will not play until the slide show is viewed.
    - A. true
    - B. false

11. If you want to create a slide with a photo and a title, you should choose _____ for the layout.
    - A. Title and Text
    - B. Title and Content
    - C. Title and Photo
    - D. Title Only

12. The Insert Picture icon will only insert a photograph.
    - A. true
    - B. false

13. The _____ key will move you forward from cell to cell in a table.
    - A. Shift
    - B. Spacebar
    - C. Tab
    - D. Enter

14. All tables are automatically created with five rows and two columns.
    - A. true
    - B. false

## BUDDY PROJECT

Open the file you created in the last chapter about the decade of your choice. Add five slides using any layout you choose. Research the following topics and create a slide for each: music, clothing, entertainment, careers, and housing.

## GUIDED PRACTICE

Open the file you started in the last chapter about your career choice. Add three slides using any layout you choose. Research the following topics and create a slide for each: job description, education requirements, and employers.

# Chapter 3

## ANIMATIONS

**Do you remember the last evening news broadcast you watched or heard?** Newscasters and reporters cover topics ranging from current events and weather to entertainment and sports. They use vocal transitions to move from topic to topic to make the information flow better. This is similar to the visual transitions used in a PowerPoint presentation to help the information on the slides flow together.

**IN THIS CHAPTER, WE WILL:**
> Add transitions from one slide to another
> Preview the slide show
> Insert an animation scheme to change the way the text appears
> View your presentation by manually advancing the slides
> Add a timer to allow the presentation to play automatically

# Lesson 3-1 TRANSITIONS

## IN THIS LESSON, WE WILL:
> Add transitions from one slide to another
> Preview the slide show

## KEY TERMS
transitions

Now that we have created our slide show, let's add some pizzazz to the presentation part of it. In this chapter, we will learn how to change the display from one slide to another by adding transitions. We will also have our text come out one bulleted point at a time by adding an animation scheme.

## TRANSITIONING FROM ONE SLIDE TO ANOTHER

**Transitions** can help build excitement for an upcoming slide as well as add closure to the previous slide. In Microsoft PowerPoint, there are over 50 different transitions from which to choose, ranging from very simple to more complex and dramatic.

1. Open **PowerPoint 2.3-About Me** that you created in the last chapter.
2. Click **File** on the menu bar and then click **Save As**.
3. Save the file as **PowerPoint 3.1-Transitions**.
4. Click **Slide Show** on the menu bar and then click **Slide Transition**.

The Slide Transition task pane opens along the right side of the screen.

Figure 3-01    The Slide Transition task pane

5. The available transitions are listed in the top portion of the task pane. When you click a transition, you see a preview of it on your slide.
6. Click **Comb Vertical**. That one is pretty cool, but let's try another.
7. Scroll down and then click **Newsflash**. That one is pretty cool, too, but let's review a few more options.
8. Scroll down a little farther and then click **Shape Diamond** once. Is it getting harder to decide on one that you like?

## IMPORTANT VOCABULARY TERMS

**transitions:** specify how the display changes as a user moves from one slide to another.

9. Scroll down a little farther and then click **Wedge**. That is the one you will use.

We can also choose the speed in which the transition will go from one slide to another.

10. Under the Modify transition sub-heading, click the Speed down arrow and then click **Medium**.

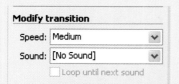

**Figure 3-02    The Modify transition section of the task pane**

So far, the Wedge transition only has been applied to that single slide. However, we want the Wedge transition to be applied to the entire slide show.

11. At the bottom of the task pane, click the **Apply to All Slides** button.

## IMPORTANT INFORMATION

You can also choose a few transitions and apply each one to the individual slide(s).

# PREVIEWING THE SLIDE SHOW

Let's take a look at what our slide show will look like with the new transition.

1. If necessary, click the first slide and then click the **Slide Show** button on the Slide Transition task pane.

**Figure 3-03    The Apply to All Slides button and the Slide Show button**

2. Click your left mouse button or press the Spacebar to advance from slide to slide.

3. When you get to the end of the slide show, you will see a black screen. Click the left mouse button again or press the **Spacebar** again to return to the Slides pane.

Great job! Your presentation is starting to look very professional.

4. Save your presentation.

## NOW YOU TRY IT!

Open the file PowerPoint 3-Extracurricular Activities from the data disk. Choose one transition and add it to the entire presentation.

Save your presentation as **Now You Try It-Lesson 3.1**.

# Lesson 3-2 ANIMATION SCHEME

**IN THIS LESSON, WE WILL:**
> Insert an animation scheme to change the way the text appears

**KEY TERMS**
animation scheme

The slides in our presentation now have good transitions from one to the other, and they add some excitement. However, we also want to add a little excitement to the text on our slides. In this lesson, we are going to add some special effects to the way the text and other objects appear on the slide.

## ANIMATION SCHEME

The **animation scheme**, which includes the preset visual effects that determine the way text and other objects appear, not only adds interest to the presentation, but also allows the speaker to control the flow of information and emphasize important points. An animation scheme also helps audience members focus on the presentation and the current topic.

1. If necessary, open **PowerPoint 3.1-Transitions** that you created in the last lesson.
2. Click **File** on the menu bar and then click **Save As**.

3. Save the file as **PowerPoint 3.2-Animation Scheme**.
4. Click **Slide Show** on the menu bar and then click **Animation Schemes**.

**TIPS & TRICKS**

You have many different animation choices from which to choose. However, just because there are over 30 different animation options does not mean you should use them all. Be aware of your audience and keep your presentation simple by choosing only one animation scheme for your entire presentation. Your information should be what people remember most, not the many animations you used.

**IMPORTANT VOCABULARY TERMS**

**animation scheme:** preset visual effects that determine the way text and other objects appear on the slide.

The Animation Schemes options appear on the Slide Design task pane.

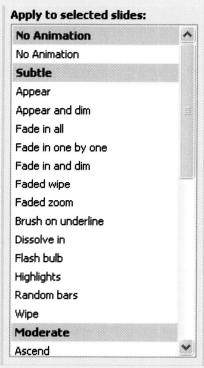

Figure 3-04    The Animation Schemes on the Slide Design task pane

5. To preview some of the animation schemes, click **Fade in one by one** under the Subtle animation sub-heading.

Watch your slide to see how the effect makes the text appear one line at a time.

6. Click **Spin** under the Moderate animation sub-heading.

That is kind of fun, but this style could become too distracting for an entire presentation.

7. Scroll down and then click **Neutron** under the Exciting animation sub-heading.

Wow! That one is pretty fun, too.

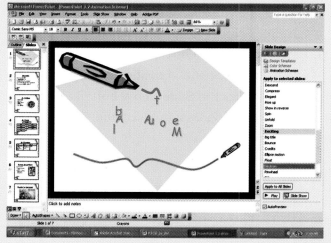

Figure 3-05    Preview of Neutron animation effect

# Lesson 3-2 ANIMATION SCHEME

Although the Neutron animation is very busy, the spinning is used only on the title. The remaining items on the slide use Rise Up as the animation. If you place your mouse pointer over the name of the animation scheme, you will see what will be used on the title and body of the slide. Sometimes it is the same effect, but as we see in the Neutron scheme, sometimes they are not the same.

Title: Neutron
Body: Rise Up

**Figure 3-06  The Animation Scheme ScreenTip**

8. To use the Neutron scheme throughout your presentation, click the **Apply to All Slides** button.
9. Before you continue, preview your presentation again to check the transitions and animation scheme. Click the **Slide Show** button at the bottom of the Slide Design task pane.

## HINTS

Remember, you advance from slide to slide and from item to item within a slide by either clicking the left mouse button or pressing the Spacebar.

10. Save your work again and then close the presentation.

## NOW YOU TRY IT!

Open the file you created at the end of the last lesson titled "Now You Try It-Lesson 3.1." Add an animation scheme to the presentation. Save the file as **Now You Try It-Lesson 3.2**.

# Lesson 3-3 VIEWING THE SLIDE SHOW

## IN THIS LESSON, WE WILL:
> View our presentation by manually advancing the slides
> Add a timer to allow the presentation to play automatically

## KEY TERMS
slide sorter view

Our slide show is nearly ready to present! We have a couple of options when viewing the slide show. We can manually advance our slides, or we can set timings so the slide show will play automatically.

## MANUALLY ADVANCING A PRESENTATION

We have already practiced with manually advancing through our slides; however, we will go through the steps again from the beginning.

1. Open **PowerPoint 3.2-Animation Scheme** that you created in the previous lesson.
2. Click **Slide Show** on the menu bar and then click **View Show**.

Your slide show will start. Remember, you can either click your left mouse button or press the spacebar to advance through the presentation. You can also press the Escape key at any point to end the slide show.

## TIPS & TRICKS
You can also press F5 to view your slide show. Another way to view it is to click View on the menu bar and then click Slide Show.

*That's it! Let's now add some timings to the presentation to allow it to play by itself.*

# Lesson 3-3 VIEWING THE SLIDE SHOW

## SETTING TIMINGS

We have decided that we would like to add timings so our presentation can play by itself without having someone advance the slides manually. This is a great option when audience members come and go. This would work great at an open house or parents' night at school.

1. Before you continue, save the file as **PowerPoint 3.3-Timings** so you can keep the previous file, which does not have the timings set, intact.
2. Click **Slide Show** on the menu bar and then click **Rehearse Timings**.

Figure 3-07    The Rehearsal timer

Your slide show will start and you will see a little Rehearsal timer in the upper-left corner.

3. Click through your presentation. Be sure to allow enough time to read each item before clicking again and advancing the Rehearse timer.

*Every time you left mouse click or space your presentation, you are setting the timings for each item or bullet. Make sure you allow enough time for the audience to read each bullet or view each item before advancing the Rehearse timer with either your mouse or the spacebar.*

4. When you finish, you will see a message telling you how long your slide show was and asking if you would like to keep the times.

Figure 3-08    The Keep Slide Timings question

5. Click the **Yes** button.

You will now see miniature slides of your entire slide show called the **Slide Sorter View**. This view allows you to see the layout of your slides and easily move them. If you need to move a slide, all you have to do is click and drag the slide to the new location.

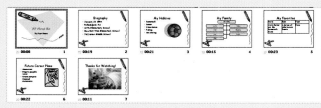

**Figure 3-09   The Slide Sorter View**

When you are in the Slide Sorter View, you will also see the exact number of seconds each slide will play. If you decide a slide does not have enough time, or if a slide has too much time, you can always change the time.

6. Click the first slide.
7. Click the **Transition** button on the toolbar.

**Figure 3-10   The Transition button on the Slide Sorter toolbar**

## IMPORTANT VOCABULARY TERMS

**slide sorter view:** way of viewing the slide show where you see all slides in miniature.

# Lesson 3-3 VIEWING THE SLIDE SHOW

The Slide Transition task pane opens along the right side of the screen.

8. Under the Advance slide heading, you can change the time allotted for this slide. Click the up or down arrow to add or subtract time for this slide.

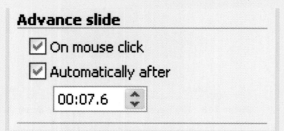

**Advance slide**
☑ On mouse click
☑ Automatically after
00:07.6

Figure 3-11    The time setting under the Advance Slide heading

9. Click the next slide and then adjust the time as necessary.
10. Continue to adjust the times as you see fit for your presentation.
11. View your slide show using one of the ways we learned earlier in this lesson.

## HINTS
You can click View and Slide Show, press the F5 button, or click Slide Show and View Show to view the presentation.

12. Sit back and enjoy the show!
13. Save your work again and then close your presentation.

## NOW YOU TRY IT!
Open the file you created at the end of the last lesson titled Now You Try It-Lesson 3.2. Set timings for the presentation to play automatically. Save the file as **Now You Try It-Lesson 3.3**.

# Chapter 3
## WRAP UP

> Transitions are used to help build excitement for upcoming slides and add closure to the previous slide.

> Different transitions can be added to different slides.

> You can advance through the slides by clicking your left mouse button or pressing the Spacebar.

> The animation scheme determines how text and other objects appear on the slide.

> Animating text helps audience members focus on the presentation and the current topic.

> It is best to choose only one animation scheme for the entire presentation so you don't overwhelm your audience.

> Timers can be set to allow the presentation to run automatically.

## WHAT DO YOU KNOW?

1. An animation scheme determines how the display changes as a user moves from one slide to another.
   A. true
   B. false

2. Microsoft PowerPoint has over 50 different transitions from which to choose.
   A. true
   B. false

# Chapter 3
## WRAP UP

3. A _____ can help build excitement for an upcoming slide as well as add closure to the previous slide.
   - A. transpose
   - B. transistor
   - C. transition
   - D. transcontinental

4. You can choose from slow, medium, and fast for the speed of the transition.
   - A. true
   - B. false

5. When you click a transition, it will automatically be applied to the entire slide show.
   - A. true
   - B. false

6. You can _____ to advance from slide to slide.
   - A. click the left mouse button
   - B. click the right mouse button
   - C. press the Spacebar
   - D. A and B
   - E. A and C

7. The _____ adds preset visual effects that determine the way text and other objects appear on the slide.
   - A. animation scheme
   - B. transition
   - C. special effects
   - D. none of the above

## PROJECT PRACTICE

Open the Language Arts project you edited in the last chapter. Add a transition and animation scheme of your choice.

Open the Math project you edited in Chapter 1. Set timings so the presentation will play automatically.

Open the Social Studies project you edited in the last chapter. Add the transition "Dissolve" to the presentation. Also add the animation scheme "Dissolve In" to the presentation. Set timings so the presentation will play automatically.

Open the Science project you edited in Chapter 1. Add a transition and animation scheme of your choice.

8. The animation scheme _____.
   A. adds interest to the presentation
   B. allows the speaker to control the flow and emphasize important points
   C. helps the audience members focus on the presentation and the current topic
   D. all of the above

9. You should use a different animation scheme on every slide to keep the presentation exciting.
   A. true
   B. false

10. You can press _____ to view the slide show.
   A. F4
   B. F5
   C. F6
   D. F7

11. You can choose to set timings to allow the presentation to play automatically.
   A. true
   B. false

12. The _____ view is when you see miniature slides of your entire slide show.
   A. Slide Sorter
   B. Outline
   C. Normal
   D. Slide Show

## BUDDY PROJECT

Open the Buddy project you edited in the last chapter. Add a transition and animation scheme of your choice. Also, set timings so the presentation will play automatically.

## GUIDED PRACTICE

Open the Guided Practice project you edited in the last chapter. Add a transition and animation scheme of your choice. Also, set timings so the presentation will play automatically.

13. You can change the amount of time each slide is shown in the _____ task pane.
    A. Slide Transition
    B. Animation Scheme
    C. Slide Layout
    D. Slide Design

14. In the Slide Sorter view, you just click and drag to move a slide.
    A. true
    B. false

15. When setting timings for the presentation, you should _____ .
    A. allow enough time for the audience to read each item
    B. click quickly to make everything appear at once
    C. count to 30 before advancing to the next line
    D. all of the above

# Chapter 4
## SOUNDS

**Have you ever yelled "Charge!" at a baseball game? Have you ever** stomped your feet and clapped your hands at a pep rally? If you have, it was probably because you were excited and you heard the sounds of an organ or the beat of the bass drum from a marching band. Music can enhance your mood, making you feel happy, excited, or even sad or glum. Some songs are upbeat and make you want to get up and dance and clap, whereas some songs are slower and help you relax. Sounds can also emphasize a presentation the way songs can enhance your mood.

IN THIS CHAPTER, WE WILL:
> Insert music from the Clip Organizer
> Format the music to play throughout the entire presentation
> Play a CD audio track
> Add a sound effect for emphasis
> Record a sound into your presentation

# Lesson 4-1 MUSIC

## IN THIS LESSON, WE WILL:
> Insert music from the Clip Organizer
> Format the music to play throughout the entire presentation
> Play a CD audio track

## KEY TERMS
looping
track

We are going to add a piece of background music that will play throughout the entire presentation. In this lesson, you will learn how to insert music from the Clip Organizer and from a CD. Music can enhance the mood of a presentation. We are hoping to find music that will complement the information in our presentation.

## ADDING MUSIC FROM THE CLIP ORGANIZER

1. Open **PowerPoint 3.3-Timings** that you created in the last chapter.
2. Click **File** on the menu bar and then click **Save As**.
3. Save the file as **PowerPoint 4.1-Music**.
4. If the presentation is still in Slide Sorter view, double-click the first slide to go back to the Normal view.

When you add music to the presentation, it is important to view the first slide because that is where you want the music to start.

5. Click **Insert** on the menu bar and point to **Movies and Sounds**.

You will see several different options for inserting sounds: from the Clip Organizer, from a saved file, play a CD, or record your own sounds.

| Movie from Clip Organizer... |
| Movie from File... |
| Sound from Clip Organizer... |
| Sound from File... |
| Play CD Audio Track... |
| Record Sound |

**Figure 4-01    Sound options on the Movies and Sounds menu**

6. Click **Sound from Clip Organizer**.
7. The Insert Clip Art task pane opens, showing only those clips that are sounds.
8. To listen to the clip, point to a clip, click the down arrow on the right side of the clip, and then click **Preview/Properties**.

The Preview/Properties dialog box opens, and the music starts to play. This dialog box also tells how the music is categorized and allows you to stop and pause the sound.

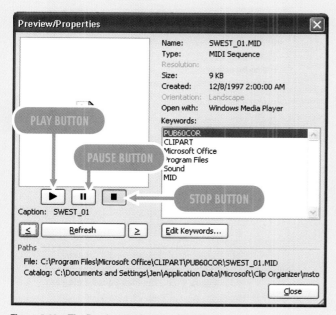

Figure 4-02  The Preview/Properties dialog box

9. After you have listened to the selection, click the **Close** button to close the dialog box.
10. Repeat steps 8 and 9 until you find a clip that you would like to insert into your presentation. Try to select one with music that fits the content of your presentation. Click the picture of the clip you have selected to insert it.

A dialog box opens asking if you want the sound clip to play automatically or to start with a mouse click.

Figure 4-03  The options to play the sound clip dialog box

11. Click the **Automatically** button.

A small, yellow speaker appears in the center of the slide. The speaker does not need to be such a big focal point of the slide.

12. Drag the speaker to one of the corners of the slide.
13. Save your presentation.

# Lesson 4-1 MUSIC

## SETTING UP THE SOUND

Even though we have entered our sound clip into the presentation, we are not quite done yet. If we were to stop now, our music would play only during the first slide. You need to change some settings to make the music play throughout the entire presentation.

1. Click the little picture of the speaker if it is not still selected.
2. Click **Slide Show** on the menu bar and then click **Custom Animation**.

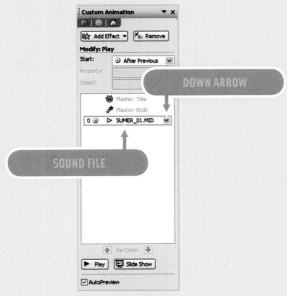

Figure 4-04   The Custom Animation task pane

The Custom Animation task pane allows you to change the order in which objects appear on the slide.

3. Click the down **arrow** next to the sound file and then click **Effect Options...**

The Play Sound dialog box opens.

Figure 4-05   The Play Sound dialog box

You need to make two changes in this dialog box. For the sound to continue playing as you advance the slides, you need to tell it when to stop. You also need to tell the music to start over again if it stops.

4. Click the **Effect** tab, if it is not already selected.
5. Under Stop Playing, click **After:** and then type **7** next to the word "slides." You type 7 because that is the total number of slides you have.
6. Click the **Timing** tab.

TIMING TAB

Figure 4-06    The Timing tab on the Play Sound dialog box

7. Click the down arrow next to the word **Repeat**. Click **Until End of Slide**.

Changing this setting makes the music play over and over until you tell it to stop. If you didn't make this change and the music was shorter than the time it took to present your slide show, it would stop.

8. Click the **OK** button.
9. Save your presentation.

# PLAY CD AUDIO TRACK DURING A PRESENTATION

Sometimes, it is nice to have a CD play instead of the musical choices from the Clip Organizer. PowerPoint gives you an option to play a CD audio track.

1. If you have a CD available and would like to play that instead, delete the little speaker on the first slide by clicking it to select it, and then pressing the **Delete** key.
2. Put your CD in the disk drive.
3. Click **Insert** on the menu bar and then point to **Movies and Sounds**.
4. Click **Play CD Audio Track**.

# Lesson 4-1 MUSIC

**looping**: making a music clip play over and over.

**track**: a song on a CD.

The Insert CD Audio dialog box will open. From this box, you can choose which track(s) to play. A **track** is a song on a CD. You can also choose to have the music play over and over if the presentation is longer than the music clip. Having a single music track play over and over is called **looping**.

**Figure 4-07    The Insert CD Audio dialog box**

5. Double-click the number in the Track: box under Start: to select it and then type the track number you have chosen. Select the Stop: track in the same way.

6. Click the **Loop until stopped** check box to select it and then click the **OK** button.

A dialog box opens asking if you want the music to play automatically or start on a mouse click.

7. Click the **Automatically** button.

A small picture of a CD appears in the center of the slide.

8. Again, you don't need this to be a focal point of the slide, so drag it to a corner of the slide.

Next you need to format this music clip similarly to the way you formatted the music from the Clip Organizer.

9. Click **Slide Show** on the menu bar and then click **Custom Animation**.

The Custom Animation task pane allows you to change the order in which objects appear on the slide.

**Figure 4-08 The Custom Animation task pane**

10. Click the down arrow next to the sound file and then click **Effect Options**.

The Play Sound dialog box opens.

You need to make one change in this dialog box. For the sound to continue playing as you advance the slides, you need to create a stopping point.

11. Click the **Effect** tab, if it is not already selected.
12. Under Stop Playing, click **After:** and then type **7** next to the word "slides."
13. Click the **OK** button.

Because this presentation is for your personal use, it is okay to use a song from a music CD. However, if you were going to show your presentation to a large audience or sell copies of your presentation, you would be restricted to the amount of music you can use. Copyright laws restrict you to using 30 seconds or 10 percent of the song—whichever is less—when a presentation is either sold or shown to a large audience. Because you are creating the presentation only for your own use, you do not need to obtain permission for using the piece of music you selected.

14. Preview your slide show.
15. Save your presentation.
16. Close your presentation.

## NOW YOU TRY IT!

Open the file you edited at the end of the last chapter titled Now You Try It-Lesson 3.3. Add a music clip from the Clip Organizer. Change the settings to make the music play throughout the entire show, making sure to loop it. Save your presentation as **Now You Try It-Lesson 4.1**.

# Lesson 4-2 SOUND EFFECTS

You found some background music and inserted it into the presentation in the last lesson. However, sometimes you are looking for a different type of sound during a slide show.

## SOUND EFFECT

A **sound effect** is a specific sound such as a dog barking, a baby crying, or a doorbell ringing. It is used primarily for a specific emphasis. It can be used in conjunction with background music. However, the sound effect is not something that you would have loop over and over; a looping sound effect would become too distracting.

1. Open **PowerPoint 4.1-Music** that you created in the previous lesson.
2. Click **File** on the menu bar and then click **Save As**.
3. Save the file as **PowerPoint 4.2-Sound Effects**.

*You want to insert two different sound effects to add emphasis to your slide show. You may choose to add slightly different sounds based on the content of your presentation.*

4. Click the third slide: **My Hobbies**.

You will add a sound effect that relates to one or more of your hobbies.

5. Click **Insert** on the menu bar and then point to **Movies and Sounds**.
6. Click **Sound from Clip Organizer**.

The Insert Clip Art task pane opens again displaying all of the sound files located on your computer.

7. Search for a specific sound, such as cheering.
8. To listen to the clip, click the down arrow on the right side and then click **Preview/Properties**.

## IMPORTANT VOCABULARY TERMS

**sound effect**: specific sound such as a dog barking or a baby crying; used primarily for a specific emphasis.

The Preview/Properties dialog box opens, and the sound effect plays. Recall that this dialog box also tells how the sound effect is categorized and allows you to stop and pause the sound.

9. After you have listened to the sound effect, click the **Close** button to close the dialog box.
10. Once you find a sound effect that you like, click the picture of the clip to insert it.

A dialog box opens asking if you want the sound effect to play automatically or start with a mouse click.

11. Click the **Automatically** button.

A small, yellow speaker appears in the center of the slide.

12. The speaker need not be such a big focal point of this slide. Drag the speaker to one of the corners of the slide like you did earlier with the music clip speaker.
13. Save your presentation.

14. Choose a different slide to add a sound effect to. You could choose to add a sound effect to the slide about your future career, your family (maybe a pet), or even your biography.
15. Insert a sound effect using the steps you just learned.
16. Save the presentation again.
17. View the slide show to hear your new sound effects.

## NOW YOU TRY IT!

Open the file you edited at the end of the last lesson titled Now You Try It-Lesson 4.1. Add one or two sound effects to help emphasize the specific clubs. Save your presentation as **Now You Try It-Lesson 4.2**.

# Lesson 4-3 RECORDING A SOUND

Our slide show is nearly finished! We have added a variety of sounds to add emphasis to the presentation. However, you are going to add one more piece of sound this time, something more personal.

## RECORDING A SOUND

The sound you are going to record is your own voice. You will introduce yourself at the beginning of the presentation. Before you begin, you will need a microphone. Your teacher will help you plug the **microphone** into the correct port of your computer.

1. Open **PowerPoint 4.2-Sound Effects** that you created in the last lesson, if it is not already open.
2. Click **File** on the menu bar and then click **Save As**.
3. Save the file as **PowerPoint 4.3-Voice**.
4. Plug your microphone into the correct port.

5. Click the first slide to view it, click **Insert** on the menu bar, and then point to **Movies and Sounds**.
6. Click **Record Sound**.

The Record Sound dialog box opens. You have the opportunity to name your sound in this dialog box.

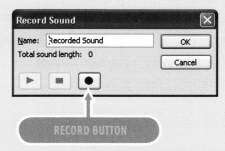

Figure 4-09    The Record Sound dialog box

## IMPORTANT VOCABULARY TERMS

**microphone:** a device used to convert sound waves (like your voice) into electric energy. The electric energy produced can then be recorded onto tape or CD.

58 | CHAPTER 4:// SOUNDS                    LESSON 4-3:// RECORDING A SOUND

7. In the Name: text box, drag to select the text and then type **Introduction** as the name of the sound.

8. Click the **Record** button, which looks like a red circle.

9. Say **"My name is (insert your name). This presentation will tell you more about me."**

10. Click the **Stop** button, which looks like a black square.

The dialog box displays the total time of your recorded sound.

11. Click the **OK** button.

Another speaker appears in the center of the slide. Drag it to a corner, too.

12. View your presentation.
13. Save your work.

*Congratulations! You should be very proud of yourself for creating such a great presentation. I hope you enjoyed the show.*

## NOW YOU TRY IT!

Open the file you edited at the end of the last lesson titled Now You Try It-Lesson 4.2. Record your voice at the beginning telling students that it is important to join an extra-curricular activity. Save your presentation as **Now You Try It-Lesson 4.3**.

# Chapter 4
## WRAP UP

> Music can be formatted to play throughout the entire presentation.
> Sounds can be inserted from the Clip Organizer, from a saved file, or off a CD. Personalized sounds can also be recorded.
> Music can be formatted to play only on certain slides.
> Looping the music will make it play over and over until it is stopped.
> Copyright laws restrict the amount of music to 30 seconds or 10 percent of the song, whichever is less, when the presentation is either sold or shown to a large audience.
> A sound effect is a specific sound added for emphasis.
> PowerPoint will allow you to record your own sound.

# WHAT DO YOU KNOW?

1. You need to view the slide where you want the sound to be inserted.
   A. true
   B. false

2. Which of the following sounds cannot be inserted into a PowerPoint presentation?
   A. sounds from the Clip Organizer
   B. saved sound files
   C. a CD audio track
   D. a recording of your own sounds
   E. All of the above can be inserted.

3. To listen to the sound clip before you insert it, click _____ .
   A. Listen/Hear
   B. Preview/Properties
   C. Sounds/Music
   D. Insert/Capture

4. When you find a sound clip you like from the Clip Organizer, you just click the icon to insert it.
   A. true
   B. false

5. The music clip will play only when you click the icon.
   A. true
   B. false

6. When a music clip is inserted from the Clip Organizer, a small _____ appears in the center of the slide.
   A. yellow speaker
   B. blue hand
   C. CD
   D. white box

7. When you insert a sound, it automatically plays throughout the entire slide show without you needing to change any settings.
   A. true
   B. false

8. When a music clip plays over and over, it is called _____ .
   A. repeating
   B. copying
   C. playing
   D. looping

## CROSS-CURRICULAR PROJECT

Open the Language Arts project you edited in the last chapter. Add a music clip that will play throughout the entire presentation.

Open the Math project you edited in the last chapter. Record your voice to explain the concepts in the presentation.

Open the Social Studies project you edited in the last chapter. Add three sound effects to emphasize the topics.

Open the Science project you edited in the last chapter. Add a music clip to play throughout the entire presentation.

9. Copyright laws restrict music usage to _____ —whichever is less.
   A. 2 minutes or 20 percent
   B. 10 seconds or 30 percent
   C. 30 seconds or 10 percent
   D. 20 seconds or 10 percent

10. A _____ is a specific sound such as a dog barking or a baby crying.
    A. music clip
    B. sound effect
    C. special effect
    D. none of the above

11. The record button is a _____ .
    A. red circle
    B. black square
    C. red arrow
    D. black arrow

12. The stop button is a _____.
    A. red circle
    B. black square
    C. red arrow
    D. black arrow

## BUDDY PROJECT

Open the Buddy project you edited in the last chapter. Add a music clip to play throughout the entire presentation. Also add two sound effects for emphasis.

## GUIDED PRACTICE

Open the Guided Practice project you edited in the last chapter. Add a music clip to play throughout the entire presentation, add at least one sound effect, and record your voice for an introduction.

# Glossary

**7x7 rule** no more than seven bullets on a slide and no more than seven words within each bulleted point.

## A

**animation scheme** preset visual effects that determine the way text and other objects appear on the slide.

## B

**bullets** small dots, dashes, or other pictures used when creating lists. They should be consistent within the list.

## C

**cell** each individual box of a table.

**clip art** drawing of an object used to add emphasis to text.

## D

**design template** preset background design with coordinating text.

## F

**Formatting toolbar** contains many shortcuts to change the appearance of your text.

**looping** making a music clip play over and over.

## M

**media clip** animated clip art or actual clip from a movie.

**menu bar** row of words across the top of the screen that when clicked reveal other commands.

**microphone** a device used to convert sound waves (like your voice) into electric energy. The electric energy produced can then be recorded onto tape or CD.

## O

**organization chart** diagram used to show the hierarchical relationship of items.

**Outline tab** method of viewing your slide show as an outline with main points and subpoints bulleted.

## P

**presentation program** software that acts like an electronic outline used to present information.

# Glossary

**slide** a screen in an electronic presentation program used to display information.

**slide sorter view** way of viewing the slide show where you will see all slides in miniature.

**Slides tab** method of viewing your slide show as miniature slides.

**sound effect** specific sound such as a dog barking or a baby crying used primarily for a specific emphasis.

**Standard toolbar** contains shortcuts for many common tools such as Open, Save, Print, and View.

**table** diagram with columns and rows used to list and compare items.

**task pane** part of the window that is used to open an existing presentation, to create a new presentation, and for searching.

**Title bar** blue bar that runs across the top of the screen that tells the name of the document as well as the name of the program used to create it.

**title slide** generally the first slide of a presentation used to tell the title of the presentation and the author(s).

**track** a song on a CD.

**transitions** specifies how the display changes as a user moves from one slide to another.

# Index

# Index

# Index

# Photo Credits

**Chapter 1:**
White male speaker uses PowerPoint
during presentation on Web marketing

**Chapter 2:**
Dinosaur named Sue on display in Chicago

**Chapter 3:**
Asian Television news reporter conducting
interview

**Chapter 4:**
Field marching band at football game